Cunard's Stateliest Ship

QUEEN MARY

VOLUME I : FROM CONCEPT TO DELIVERY

A Pictorial Record from Contemporary Sources

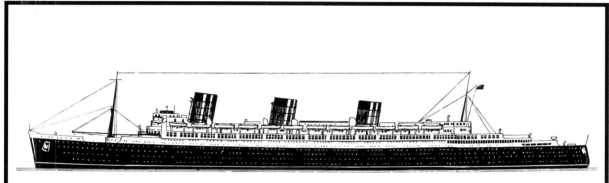

E.C. Talbot-Booth, 1944

First in a series covering the design, development and career of Queen Mary, with each stage of her career carefully illustrated and detailed.

R.A. & L. Streater

with additional research material from D. Greenman

the maritime publishing company

We would like to acknowledge the great help and assistance received
during the preparation of this book from:
David Greenman (Editor, Jane's Merchant Ships);
the staff at the Cunard Archives, Liverpool University;
the Keepers of the Records of Scotland; the Librarian and Staff
at the National Maritime Museum, Greenwich;
Tony Smith (World Ship Society),
Martin Cox and members of the "Liners" group,
Julian Hill and members of the "Queen Mary" group,
Maritime History group, John Barkhurst, Kevin Tam,
Charles Dragonette and Bruce Vancil (all on the Internet)
and of course our respective families

in association with
B. Harvey

Printing by:
Ashford Colour, Gosport PO12 4DT

Published by

the maritime publishing company

Jasmine Lodge, 1 Highfield Close, Canterbury, Kent CT2 9DZ, UK
Telephone: 01227 780259 : Facsimile: 01227 454992
e-mail: marpubco@junk1234.demon.co.uk :
http://www.junk1234.demon.co.uk

Cunard's
QUEEN MARY

from a picture by Frank Mason, courtesy of Cunard Archives, Liverpool University

Length overall	1019ft 6in
Length between perpendiculars	965ft 0in
Breadth moulded	118ft 0in
Depth moulded	92ft 6in
Gross tonnage	80,774 tons
Net tonnage	34,118 tons
Displacement	81,237 tons
Draught corresponding	38ft 10in
Designed shaft horsepower	212,000
Designed service speed	28·5 knots
Passengers:	2,139
Cabin class	740 (+36)
Tourist class	760 (+24)
Third class	579
Crew	1,101

THE STATELIEST SHIP

The introduction of controls on US immigration in the early twenties altered forever the high profits that so many shipping lines had been making from carrying the vast numbers of European immigrants to their new life in a new country.

In the late twenties the directors of Cunard began to consider their future plans. At that time their express service was using *Mauretania* (1907), *Berengaria* (1912) and *Aquitania* (1914), but times and tastes had moved on. Cunard's board decided it was time to have a fresh look at the needs of the trans-Atlantic passenger.

New materials and technology meant that it was now possible to maintain a weekly schedule with two liners rather than the three as previously required. Cunard's in-house design team prepared draft sketches for a proposed superliner of around a thousand feet long. This was put before the directors, who then began to seriously consider the project and its potential.

The growing use of fuel oil rather than coal, and the rapid development of new engine technology, meant that a new liner could maintain the minimum speed that would be necessary to achieve a two-liner crack service – at least 28 knots as an average, but with more power in reserve to make up any time lost through bad weather.

Another advantage of fuel oil meant that the liner could be re-fuelled in a fraction of the time needed for coaling, with none of the problems of coal dust drifting throughout the vessel, necessitating thorough cleaning before the next contingent of passengers could be allowed on board. This drastically reduced the time needed in port.

By 1929 the Cunard directors had finalised their ideas and put out invitations to various shipyards to tender to build the new liner. The successful bid came from John Brown on the Clyde. They had built several successful ships for Cunard in the preceding thirty years, including *Saxonia*, *Caronia*, *Carmania*, *Lusitania*, *Aquitania*, *Franconia* and *Alaunia*. The two companies enjoyed a good working relationship, which would be crucial in a project of such enormity.

In particular, they were prepared to build and fit the entire ship, taking overall responsibility for the total project, whereas other yards that put in tenders were proposing to sub-contract out much of the work.

The contract was placed with John Brown's on 1st December, 1930, and was listed on their books as Hull No. 534, by which name it was to be known for the next four years – the final name was to be one of the best-kept secrets in the maritime world and a source of many tales.

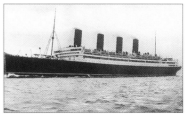

Cunard's crack express service was operated by Berengaria *(top),* Mauretania *(centre) and* Aquitania *(lower).*

Some of John Brown's other liners for Cunard included: Carmania *(top);* Caronia *(centre); and* Alaunia *(bottom).*

One of the models shown here in the testing tank at John Brown's shipyard. A motorised gantry towed the models up and down the tank at various speeds, with a wide range of simulated Atlantic conditions, during thousands of carefully monitored experiments. Following analysis of the results, a self-powered model was built to assess the final design.

Below left: the final model is shown here in the wind tunnel, undergoing smoke and slipstream tests.

Below is an aerial view of the entire yard, showing the railway lines, workshops and slips.

Before the design could be finalised, research and experimentation had been conducted to develop the optimum design. John Brown's Shipyard had a purpose-built testing tank at their Clydebank yard; this was 400 feet long and 20 feet wide, fully equipped with model-making facilities, electrically operated trolleys and wave-making equipment to simulate all conditions likely to be met. They had placed these facilities at Cunard's disposal in the late twenties, when the design team had been investigating the basic concepts.

To find the best hull form for the North Atlantic, twenty-two wax models were made, each around seventeen feet long. These were run up and down the tank in all manner of simulated waves, for several thousand carefully monitored experiments. Many were filmed for later thorough analysis, using around 2,400 feet of 16mm ciné film.

Further tests were conducted on various propeller designs to achieve the best compromise between the underwater hull shape and the required engine power, for the best speed and the lowest drag factor. After analysing these results and observations, a final scale model of the proposed design was built, some eighteen feet long. This model was used in the testing tank to confirm the design parameters, and was also used in wind tunnel tests to adjust the streamlining.

Further tests in the wind-tunnel helped determine the optimum height and spacing of the funnels to prevent smoke and fumes falling on the passengers.

Other tests included determining the size and positioning of the bilge keels, to keep the new liner as stable as possible.

From all these experiments, tests and analyses, the final design for Cunard's new superliner was agreed.

While the design engineers were preparing the final designs, John Brown prepared their yard and the slip, ready for the largest vessel constructed to date.

The Yard had a 3,200 foot frontage on the North Bank of the River Clyde. The Fitting Out basin was in the centre, with construction yards either side. There were five slips in the East Section, and a further three slips in the West Section. The Yard had its own machine shops, boiler shops and engineering works with associated blacksmiths and iron and brass foundries, and most of the other facilities needed. The owners also owned a nearby colliery, with a guaranteed supply of fuel.

The slip chosen for the new liner was the end one in the West Section. It needed a lot of preparation – it had to be lengthened and reinforced to take the massive hull as it was built. Millions of cubic yards of soil were removed, and support facilities improved. Eventually everything was ready.

The first keel plate was officially laid on 27th December, 1930. Construction was underway at last.

Above: The massive double bottom was around six feet deep. It was used to hold boiler feed water, ballast, and water for domestic uses.

Right: Ten million rivets were used – a total of 4,000 tons, enough to stretch from London to Newcastle. The first rivet was driven by Donald Skiffington, the shipyard director, who started as an apprentice at the yard.

Below: A view of the stern, showing the size of the casting for the shaft bosses, which would eventually take the propeller shafts.

This picture was taken from what will be the boiler rooms, looking forward. The tanks at the sides, still under construction, will be for the fuel oil.

The enormous ribs are slowly taking shape, as the outline of the hull is built up. The height of the cranes gives some idea of the size of the vessel even at this early stage. With no decks yet in place, long timber props are used to keep the correct profile. In this side view of the after end some of the side framing can be seen.

The decks are slowly being built, in the foreground; further back the size of the bulkheads can be judged.

In the picture on the right the heavy beams can be seen that will span the machinery area.

The bow starts to take on its striking shape as the ribs are completed.

The sheer size of the hull meant that the bows were built over a main service road and rail lines. A supporting bridge had to be built to enable access to be continued through the yard

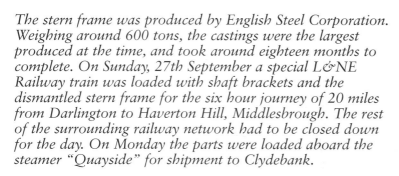

The stern frame was produced by English Steel Corporation. Weighing around 600 tons, the castings were the largest produced at the time, and took around eighteen months to complete. On Sunday, 27th September a special L&NE Railway train was loaded with shaft brackets and the dismantled stern frame for the six hour journey of 20 miles from Darlington to Haverton Hill, Middlesbrough. The rest of the surrounding railway network had to be closed down for the day. On Monday the parts were loaded aboard the steamer "Quayside" for shipment to Clydebank.

Once the castings had been assembled and incorporated into the stern, the frames and plating were completed.

By the end of 1934 the cruiser stern was finished – fully plated and ready for final painting – already the first layers of paint had been applied here. Although the propellers had been fitted by this time, there were still no engines.

Plating is progressing steadily through this series of pictures.

The ramp to the left of the hull in the bottom picture was for the workmen's access.

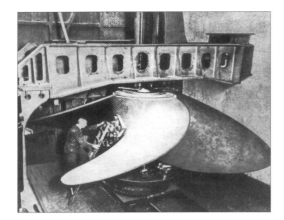

Each propeller was nearly 20 feet in diameter. Two sets were produced by two different London foundries, and each were machined and polished to perfection. Craftsmen carefully mounted each propeller before fitting the finishing boss to complete the assembly.

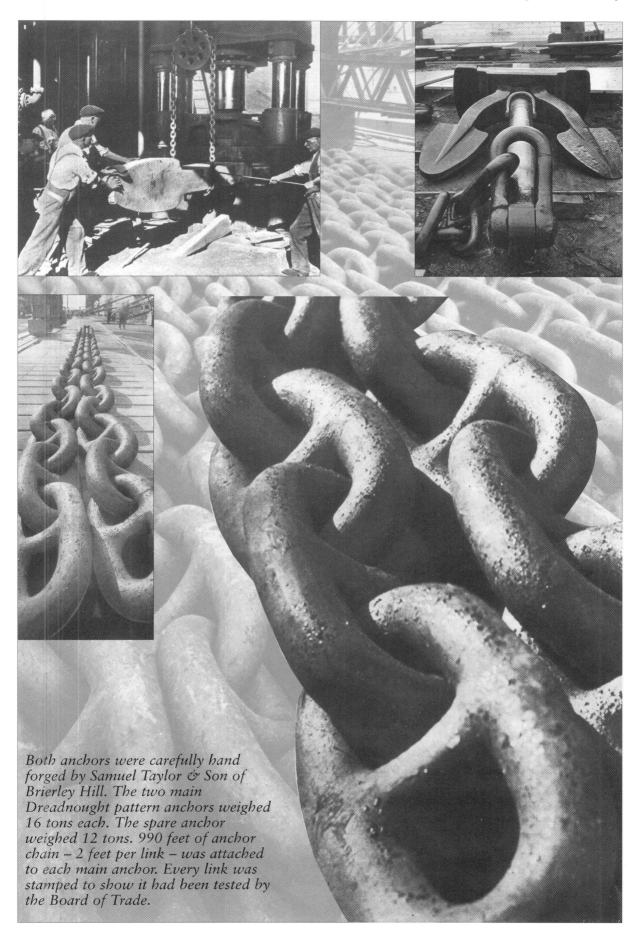

Both anchors were carefully hand forged by Samuel Taylor & Son of Brierley Hill. The two main Dreadnought pattern anchors weighed 16 tons each. The spare anchor weighed 12 tons. 990 feet of anchor chain – 2 feet per link – was attached to each main anchor. Every link was stamped to show it had been tested by the Board of Trade.

Following the slump of the Great Depression, all work on the hull was halted. The hull and the cranes loomed over the town as symbols of the depressed state of the country.

Repeated attempts were made by Cunard to obtain assistance from the Government to enable the company to complete the liner and to continue operating, but with no success. The local Member of Parliament, David Kirkwood, agitated long, loud and hard on behalf of the laid-off workers.

Eventually, on 12th December, 1933, agreement for support was reached.

Over the ensuing months the hull steadily grew, dwarfing everything around it.

The keel was laid, then ribs, beams, plating . . . all carefully designed, calculated and constructed like some monster jigsaw puzzle. As work progressed, the craftsmen steadily moved ahead of schedule: Sir Percy Bates, the Chairman of Cunard, revised his estimates, and began to plan for the new liner to be ready by the summer of 1933.

The hull was divided by eighteen watertight transverse bulkheads. The double bottom ran the entire length of the hull, and was divided into seventy compartments, about six feet high. The inner skin created an effective inner hull. Every possible safety precaution was taken.

Some ten million rivets were used throughout her construction – some 4,000 tons just for the rivets! The holes for the rivets were drilled to very carefully calculated positions, ready to take the interior bulkheads as they were installed.

The stern castings – weighing around 190 tons – were brought by rail and steamer to the yard, as they were too large and too complex to be produced on site. This necessitated closing down the railway system in the area for a day while the castings were slowly transported twenty miles from Darlington to Middlesbrough, then shipped on by steamer.

By November 1931 the hull was approximately 80% complete.

However, the world-wide Great Depression was biting ever-deeper. The emigrant traffic was shrinking rapidly, and sources of major finance were getting harder to find.

The French approached Britain, Italy and Germany to see if the countries could agree to suspend work on their rival liners, but negotiations broke down, and the French government pressed on with what was to become *Normandie*.

Then, on 11th December, 1931, Cunard abruptly called a halt to any further work on the hull. Of the thousands of men directly employed, all but a few were paid off for an undefined period. Some were kept on for essential maintenance, such as applying a thorough coating of a newly-developed anti-rust compound, but overall nearly four thousand men were laid off in the Yard, with probably another ten thousand in allied industries and suppliers. The hull was abandoned to the seagulls and the starlings and the rooks.

For the next two years the giant hull loomed over the Clyde, and symbolised for the whole nation the depth of the Depression.

The local Member of Parliament, David Kirkwood, raised the issue of No. 534 at Westminster whenever he could, but the Government consistently refused to be drawn in to the debate, refusing all entreaties to subsidise the completion of the liner.

An aerial view of the hull as it sat forlornly on the stocks during the long lay-off

With an unfortunate piece of timing, Cunard issued a special souvenir edition of their house magazine in Christmas 1931, celebrating the construction of their new liner.

Rumours had circulated for some time about a possible merger between Cunard and the White Star Line, the latter itself in serious financial difficulties.

Several attempts had been made to reach an agreement between Cunard, White Star and the Government, but all failed. Then, in October 1932, the Chancellor of the Exchequer, Neville Chamberlain, asked Lord Weir to look into the matter. Rather than form a committee, he investigated the whole problem himself, and within eight weeks had produced a report for the Government, highlighting – amongst other items – the degree of state assistance provided by most of the competitive nations currently building new liners.

As a result, the Government hammered out an agreement. Cunard and White Star were to merge into a new company, with a combined fleet, to be called The Cunard-White Star Steamship Line. Cunard received 62% of the assets of the new company, the government of Northern Ireland received 22·8%, and the trustees for the debenture shareholders of White Star received 15·2%. Once this was completed, the Government would provide £3 million, as a repayable loan, to complete No. 534, plus £1.5 million to help offset the running costs of the new line for an agreed period, and £5 million to cover the projected costs of building a further ship. This was not popular with many of the MPs at the Houses of Parliament, but was eventually agreed, and the Bill was approved on 27th March, 1934.

On the 3rd April, 1934, after 27 months of enforced idleness, the first of the workers, some 400 men, returned to the yard, flamboyantly escorted by pipers in full regalia.

The first thing they had to do was clean off the rust – around 130 tons of it. However, once the surveyors had inspected the structure, they reported that overall the state of the steelwork was quite remarkable.

The other major concern was whether or not the hull had suffered any distortion from sitting on the stocks for so long. To everyone's relief, the careful preparation of the yard prior to beginning the construction had been sufficiently thorough to support the hull throughout the period of enforced idleness.

Pipers from the Dalmuir Pipe Band prepare to lead the first of the workers back in to the yard on the resumption of work.

On 26th May, 1934, official permission was received to resume construction. Soon thousands of men were back at work, in the yard and at the many outside suppliers. Work pressed on at great speed, as the men were determined to prove their value. The Great Depression was finally lifting.

By the time the hull was completed, some 35,000 tons of steel were in place. The stern frame alone was 190 tons, and the rudder weighed in at 180 tons. The four propellers weighed 35 tons each.

Finally ready for the launch, these two views show how the hull soared majestically over the canopied launching platform. In the lower picture, the crowd can be seen massing before the platform, in front of King George V and Queen Mary. Spectators arrived throughout the day within the shipyard, in spite of the pouring rain and the biting wind.

In both pictures the cables linking to the drag chains can be clearly seen. The cables and drag chains had been carefully calulated for position, strength and weight to ensure the safe launching of the enormous hull. The result of several years of experimentation and calculations resulted in the hull stopping within two feet of the expected position.

The date for the launch was finally announced – Wednesday, 26th September, 1934. However, the name was still not released, in spite of intense speculation.

Engineers spent a long time on the calculations required to ensure a safe launch – the number and length of drag chains and where they were to be fixed, the amount and composition of grease on the slipways, etc. Directly opposite the slip was the River Cart, a tributary of the Clyde, which had been widened and deepened when *Aquitania* was launched; now further work was put in hand to give extra clearance.

The drag chains – some 2,350 tons of them – were carefully coiled under the hull at strategic points, and attached by steel hawsers to lugs welded to the hull. The slipways were coated with a slippery mixture of Tallene, plus a layer of sperm oil and soft soap. Most of the timber props under the hull were removed, until the barest minimum were left.

On the Clyde, the day had been declared a public holiday for all. Throughout the day the rain poured down. In spite of this, thousands of people filled the yards, the banks either side of the yard and the bank on the other side of the yard. Special trains were laid on to bring in many of the spectators. Grandstands were built in the fields opposite the Yard, and for weeks before people were booking seats at fifteen shillings each. Some estimates claimed around a quarter of a million people watched the events that day on the Clyde.

King George V, Queen Mary and the Prince of Wales were present for the ceremony. The King had agreed to make the speech, whilst the Queen was to actually launch the ship. A launch platform was built, with a glass fronted central section. The ceremony was to be broadcast worldwide.

In his speech, regarded by many as one the best of his reign, the King said: ". . . today we come to the happy task of sending on her way the stateliest ship now in being . . ." The soubriquet stuck, and for the rest of her life she was known as "The Stateliest Ship" to all.

At 3.10pm, following the King's speech, Queen Mary stepped forward, and finally revealed the name of the vessel: *"I am happy to name this ship Queen Mary. I wish success to her and to all who sail on her."*

The Queen then cut a pink ribbon, releasing a bottle of Australian wine to smash against the bows. She next pressed a button, which released six triggers that by now were effectively the only things restraining the hull on the slips. A second button, when pressed, operated six hydraulic rams which started to push the hull on its way. For some 24 seconds nothing happened. Then, slowly, she started to move, slowly at first, then with increasing speed. The drag chains worked exactly as predicted – the hull stopped within 2 feet of the expected point. Total time for the launch was 112 seconds; overall the ceremony had taken barely 15 minutes.

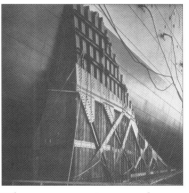

The two top pictures show over 2,000 tons of drag chains being piled in carefully designed locations ready for the launch.

The lower picture shows the fore poppet supporting the bow before the launch.

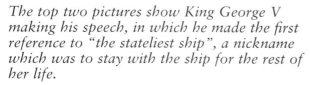

The top two pictures show King George V making his speech, in which he made the first reference to "the stateliest ship", a nickname which was to stay with the ship for the rest of her life.

In the lower picture, with King George V to her right, Queen Mary pressed the button to release the hull down the slips, and to reveal over the radio the name of the vessel to the world.

King George V stepped to the front of the launching platform, and gravely saluted the new liner as she majestically moved down the slips and gracefully entered the waters of the Clyde for the first time.

The crowd surrounding the platform applauded him and The Queen as enthusiastically as they did the new liner.

Already well down the slips, the hull almost appeared to be saluted by the attendant cranes.

150 tons of tallow and 50 tons of soft soap were used to coat the ways, to ensure the massive hull moved smoothly down the slipway into the Clyde.

As the hull hit the water, the cables started to pull on the piled drag chains, already slowing her down.

The yard was packed with spectators, with many people even climbing the cranes to get a better view.

As soon as the hull had come to a halt, the tugs quickly took her under control and then gently eased her into the fitting out basin.

Tugs swiftly moved in and took control of the hull. In spite of a freshening wind, she was quickly but carefully towed to the fitting out basin, to the west of the slip, where she would remain for the next eighteen months.

As launched the hull weighed some 35,000 tons. To maintain structural integrity during the launch, the windows in the promenade deck had not been cut out, and steel and wooden beams had been fixed inside as additional bracing.

Once in the fitting bay, many of the beams were used as protective piles against the risk of anything running into the stern, which projected some 100 feet beyond the end of the fitting out berth.

Although far and away John Brown's largest contract, this picture shows that other work was also progressing through the yard, both naval and merchant.

Thousands of craftsmen were now involved in erecting the upper decks, installing the machinery and the engines, fitting out the cabins, and installing the radio system, and the myriad other jobs.

Queen Mary was always immediately distinguishable by her three magnificent funnels. The fore funnel was some 184 feet above the keel, or 70 feet above the boat deck. The second and third funnels were progressively lower, with some 138 feet between each pair. Two Tyfon sirens, each over 6 feet long and weighing one ton apiece, were fitted to the first funnel, and another to the middle funnel. These were keyed to lower base A, or two octaves below middle A. The sound could be heard ten miles away, yet the sirens had been designed such that the passengers were never distressed.

Slowly the interiors took shape, until eventually they were ready for the artists and the interior designers to move in. The best had been chosen, preparing paintings, sculptures, carvings, stained glass fittings and other features to be used throughout the vessel.

While all this was going on, Cunard-White Star notified the Atlantic Conference, which regulated the fares used by companies operating on the North Atlantic, that they intended to classify *Queen Mary* as 'Cabin Class' rather than 'First Class'. This would enable them to fix their fares at a lower rate than on *Normandie* and other vessels. Naturally the other lines protested. Following a series of protests and appeals, the Conference decided once and for all to abolish the Cabin Class category, grouping the luxury liners together on a more equitable basis for all.

On 5th March 1936 King Edward VIII (formerly the Prince of Wales) paid an extended tour of inspection. He not only visited the Cabin Class areas as planned, he then insisted on touring the rest of the ship including the third class and the crew's quarters. In all he spent over three hours aboard.

When the King and his party left the ship, the sirens sounded for the first time, in salute to the occasion.

These two pages show the hull as it gradually took shape: the most notable feature being the three enormous funnels.

The funnels were 70, 65 and 60 feet above deck level and were built in sections. Lower left picture shows the final section of the after funnel being lowered into position.

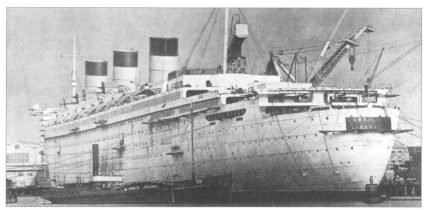

Above: fitting out, and installing all the machinery, involved thousands of workers. Some of them can be seen here leaving at the end of their shift.

Access to the centrally-heated crow's nest, 130 feet above sea level, was up this inside ladder – all 110 steps up!!! It was roofed over and fitted with a weather screen.

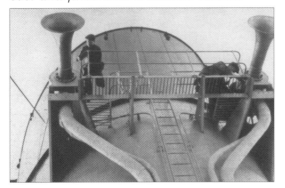

The two Tyfon sirens in the final stages of being fitted to the fore funnel. The sheer size of these sirens can be judged against the two fitters working on them.

King Edward VIII, seen here leaving the ship after his thorough trip on 5th March 1936.

Accompanied by Donald Skiffington, the shipyard director, King Edward toured the entire ship.

Queen Mary can be seen here in all her glory, as the final touches are put to her. Several lifeboats have been mounted, which were removed before she travelled down the Clyde.

Above are two interesting views contrasting the two worlds that existed even in the 1930s.

The farm worker continues his age-old traditional method of working in spite of the greatest marvel of his day sitting just behind him.

The starboard outer shaft turbine and gearing

Two of the Yarrow-type water-tube boilers

Turbogenerators produce the electrical needs

Control panels are throughout the engine room

A view across one of the main engine rooms

One of the main engine room starting platforms

The heart of the ship was the engine room. This was centred around four sets of Parson's single reduction geared turbines, four to each of the four propellers. Each turbine set had 257,000 blades, all hand-made and hand-fitted. Power output per turbine set was 50,000 horse power, turning at 3,000 revolutions per minute. Fourteen foot diameter reduction gears reduced this to 200 revolutions per minute. Each turbine set comprised one high pressure, one low pressure and two intermediate pressure turbines.

Two turbine sets were in the forward engine room, for the two outer propellers, while the aft engine room turbines were for the inner propellers.

There were twenty four Yarrow-type water tube boilers in four boiler rooms, generating steam at 400 lb/sq.in and 700°F. Number 3 and Number 5 boiler rooms fed the aft engine room, whilst Numbers 2 and 4 fed the forward engine room. Oil fuel was contained in the side bunkers, which held some 6,300 tons. There were six refuelling points around the ship, enabling refuelling to be completed in eight hours.

In the Number One boiler room were three double-ended Scotch boilers providing low pressure steam for the ancillary services such as heating and cooking.

Electricity was provided by seven turbo-generators, of over 1,300kW each, generating a total of 10,000kW/h, for the lighting, lifts, and all the other amenities expected by passengers on a modern liner, in addition to the complex needs of the marine engineering equipment such as the navigation equipment, radios, winches, steering gear and capstans. It was estimated that over 4,000 miles of electric wiring was installed throughout the liner.

The four propellers were cast in manganese bronze, in two foundries in London, and were delivered to the Yard by sea. Each one cost £7,000, weighed 35 tons, and measured 20 feet across. Yet once installed, they were each so perfectly machined, polished and balanced that they could be turned by hand.

As a precaution, apart from the main set, a second complete set was made and held in reserve.

The anchors weighed around 16 tons each, and were of an all-forged Dreadnought pattern. The two anchor chains were 165 fathoms each of high tensile steel, the links being electrically welded and fully tested. Total weight of the anchor cable was 150 tons.

The electro-hydraulic steering gear used four cast-steel hydraulic cylinders, operating in pairs on either side of the rudder. The rudder was of an unbalanced, streamlined design, and weighed around 180 tons. The rudder stock weighed 90 tons.

The electro-hydraulic steering gear under test prior to installation

The Cocktail Bar and Observation Lounge. The viewing windows looked out over the bows of the vessel and across the expanse of ocean, giving magnificent views.

Two views of the Main Restaurant – rising through an astonishing three decks.

The Main Lounge, central meeting point for the Cabin Class passengers.

Right: The Cabin Class Smoking Room.

Right: Cabin Lounge, Promenade Deck

Left: the Shopping Centre in the Main Hall on the Promenade Deck.

The Cabin Class Main Lounge was decorated principally in Canadian maple. It was designed to be used as a lounge, but could readily be adapted into a cinema or a theatre for up to 400 patrons.

"Brilliant in conception and elegant in execution, the passenger spaces reveal, down to their smallest detail, a fine appreciation of aesthetic fitness. Not a harsh note is struck anywhere." –

The Shipbuilder and Marine Engine-Builder, June 1936

Much of the furniture and the panelling was produced by the skilled workmen at the Waring and Gillows factory

CABIN CLASS PUBLIC ROOMS

The public rooms were mainly on the Promenade Deck, with the Restaurant on C Deck. The central point was the Main Hall, which included a shopping arcade, with shops operated by Austin Reed and W.H. Smith and a third unit operated by the owners, selling tobacco etc.; there were also 24 showcases used to display jewellery, souvenirs, and such, plus two small side shops.

The arcade was at the head of the main stairway, which also had four main lifts for the passengers. There was also access either side to the covered promenade areas. Other rooms that led directly off the Main Hall included the Library, a Lecture Room, a Children's Playroom, a Music Studio and a Drawing Room.

Running from the after end of either side of the Main Hall were two writing rooms, 32 feet long, which connected with the Main Lounge. This was the focus of the social scene for Cabin Class passengersboth during the day and in the evenings, and was 96 feet long by 70 feet wide, rising in the centre to nearly 30 feet high.

The port side of the Main Lounge led, via a small anteroom, to the Long Gallery, 118 feet long by 20 feet wide. This was used as an informal meeting area between passengers. Two sets of double doors opened on to the main Ballroom.

The starboard side of the Main Lounge led, via another small room, to the Starboard Gallery, which was designed as an informal smoking room for use by ladies as well as gentlemen, and connected to the side of the ballroom, for which it could be used as a quiet lounge in the evenings, during the dances.

The Ballroom was a grand spectacle, especially of an evening, with the passengers in full evening dress and the lights blazing off the golden decor. Overall the ballroom was 35 feet long by 50 feet wide, with an oak parquet dance floor 30 feet long by 34 feet wide. On the outboard end there was a raised platform where dancers could sit out and take refreshments, whilst at the other end was a similar, smaller raised platform for the orchestra.

Aft of the Ballroom was the Smoking Room. This was 42 feet by 69 feet, rising through two decks and was topped by a dome, giving an overall height of 22 feet. Decorated in much the same way as a Gentleman's Club of the period, including stuffed leather armchairs, it featured a real, coal-burning fire.

Corridors led foward off either side of the forward end of the Main Lounge to the Observation Lounge and Cocktail Bar. This was a semi-circular room; at the forward end there was a raised platform giving spectacular views from ahead to either side. At the after end of the Lounge was the

The plaque of Queen Mary, mounted at the head of the stairway to the Main Hall

The Cabin Class entrance on the Main Deck

Cocktail Bar, which was popular during the day and early evenings as an informal meeting area.

Above the Promenade Deck was the Sun Deck, at the after end of which was the Verandah Grill. This could be used as an alternative to the Main Restaurant for those choosing à la carte meals. In the evening it operated as a cocktail bar with a supper service. It also had a small sycamore parquet dance floor.

CABIN CLASS STATEROOMS

Cabin Class staterooms were arranged on the Sun, the Main, A and B Decks. Wherever possible these rooms were built outboard, and were of an 'L' shape, to gain as much natural light and ventilation as possible.

There were a number of private suites available, each of which had a sitting room and a bedroom, plus servant's room, box room and bathroom.

On A Deck there was a selection of Special Suites; these had a bedroom, sitting room, bathroom, etc., but the sitting room could also be converted into an extra bedroom .

TOURIST CLASS PUBLIC ROOMS

The main entrance and stairway served 8 levels, from the Promenade Deck to F Deck. There was an additional after staircase which covered the five accommodation decks, A to E. At the main staircase were two lifts, plus a further passenger lift beside the after staircase.

The Smoking Room on the Promenade Deck measured 42 feet long by 70 feet wide, and was furnished with a variety of settees and deep armchairs as well as a selection of chairs and small tables.

The Main Lounge, on the Main Deck, was the centre of social life for the Tourist Class. It measured 80 feet long by

A painting completed by Doris Zinkeisen, for the Verandah Grill, illustrating pantomime and circus themes.

One of four panels by Anna Zinkeisen for the Ballroom, illustrating the four seasons. This one was of 'Autumn'.

70 feet wide, and included a parquet dance floor 33 feet long by 28 feet wide, with a height over the dance floor of 16 feet. There was a stage at the after end, 20 feet long by 8 feet deep, which could also be adapted for use as a cinema, when it could seat 388 passengers.

Just forward of the Lounge were two rooms – on the port side was a Library and Writing Room, and on the starboard was a Children's Playroom. Between these two rooms was a Cocktail Bar, which was 27 feet long by 15 feet wide.

There was an additional lounge on A Deck, 56 feet long by 52 feet wide. This incorporated an oak dance floor that was 25 feet by 20 feet.

The Dining Saloon was on C Deck. It ran the full width of the ship, was 78 feet long and could seat 400 passengers.

TOURIST CLASS STATEROOMS

The staterooms were all aft, spread over A to E Decks, and were in a variety of configurations. Rooms were intended for two, three or four passengers, plus some single rooms.

THIRD CLASS PUBLIC ROOMS

Third Class passengers had their own entrance and staircase, with a passenger lift.

On the Main Deck, immediately below the bridge, was the Garden Lounge. This semi-circular room was 80 feet wide by 35 feet long. The large feature windows afforded splendid views forward.

The Smoking Room, on A Deck, was also semi-circular, although well forward of the Garden Lounge. The sweeping windows gave splendid views forward and to the side. The room was 80 feet wide and 60 feet long, and had a variety of seating arrangements. There were several recessed seating areas at the side.

The Lounge, to one side of the central entrance, was on B Deck, and was 60 feet long by 30 feet wide. On the other side of the double doors of the Lounge was a cinema of similar proportions. This also had a stage at one end for use as a theatre.

Immediately aft of the cinema was the children's playroom, well stocked with a variety of toys, a rocking horse and other facilities.

As with the other classes, the Dining Saloon was on C Deck. Capable of accommodating 412 people, it ran the full width of the ship, and was 90 feet long.

THIRD CLASS ACCOMMODATION

Arranged well-forward on D and E Decks, the Third Class accommodation was for either two or four berths. Even these rooms were equipped with fitted wardrobes, seats and hand-basins with hot and cold water.

Top left is a view of the Main Lounge; top right: meals could be taken in the Verandah Grill, which included a grand piano and a dance floor; central: the Observation Lounge and Cocktail Bar; two lower pictures: views of the Cabin Class Main Hall and the Shopping Centre.

The fireplace in the Main Lounge, above. The overall theme was golden – the tone of the wall panelling, the mantel pieces were golden onyx and all metal work was a dull gold.

The Main Lounge also had a large stage at the after end, around 26 feet wide by 22 feet deep, which was used for nightly entertainment. The carpets could be rolled back to create a beautiful ballroom.

Above: the Staboard Gallery. Left: panelling in a corner of the Smoking Room. Below: three views of the Long Gallery. The double doors at the far end opened on to the Lounge, while the side windows looked on to the Promenade Deck.

The magnificent Cabin Class restaurant. Overall length was 143 feet, including two private dining rooms at the forward end. There were two further permanent private dining rooms at the after end. Capacity was 815 people – the entire Cabin Class complement could be accommodated in one sitting!

The decorative map, which was such a prominent feature of the restaurant, was 24 feet by 15 feet. Designed by Macdonald Gill, it represented the North Atlantic and the various routes across it. A crystal model of the ship moved across the relevant route to show passengers at all times their approximate position.

To the right and below is the Tourist Class Lounge, on A Deck. There was a stage at the after end. The lounge could also be used as a cinema, capable of taking 388 people.

To the right and below are two views of the Tourist Class Dining Room, which ran the full width of the ship. It could accommodate 400 people in one sitting.

Lower right: the cocktail time dance salon, with murals by Anna Zinkeisen

The Third Class Entrance Hall on C Deck

The Third Class Garden Lounge, on the Main Deck, was a semi-circular room. Sited just below the bridge, the main panoramic windows had excellent views forward

The Third Class Smoking Room, on A Deck, was semi-circular, with wide viewing windows facing forward.

The Third Class Dining Saloon, on C Deck, ran the full width of the ship, and could accommodate some 412 people in a variety of seating configurations.

Above: private suites included their own exclusive sitting rooms, each individually decorated

Right: a first class stateroom – this one is wood lined in weathered sycamore

Below: the staterooms were mainly 'L' shaped, combining the bedroom and a sitting room, generally with their own bathroom; natural light and ventilation were used where possible as most of these rooms were outboard.

Above are two different Tourist Class bedrooms. Although of a more spartan design, the right hand cabin is still luxurious and well-fitted.

The central picture is of a typical four-berth Third Class bedroom.

To keep children happy while their parents enjoyed the crossing, Queen Mary offered three playrooms, one (lower left) for the Cabin Class, and one (lower right) for the Tourist Class, plus another for the Third Class. These playrooms were well-equipped, and well-staffed with trained nursery staff.

Top: the Cabin Class swiming pool incorporated a glass and mother of pearl ceiling. The overall room was 60 feet by 42 feet: the actual pool was 35 feet by 22 feet.

Above: the Tourist Class swimming pool on F Deck was 47 feet by 40 feet: the actual pool was 33 feet by 21 feet.

Left above: the Cabin Class gymnasium, on the Sun Deck, was 36 feet by 20 feet. Equipment included several riding machines, cycling machines, rowing machines, punch balls and a variety of other devices. Next door was a full-sized squash-racket court.

Left lower: the Tourist Class gymnasium, on F Deck, was 39 feet long by 20 feet wide, and was similarly equipped.

Throughout the ship the interiors were strikingly detailed by the best contemporary artists.

Four bronze lighting sconces depicting playing card characters in the Smoking Room.

These two paintings show historical maritime monets: to the left is Samuel Pepys when Secretary to the Admiralty; to the right is Richard Hakluyt, the naval historian, recording the voyages of Elizabethan sailors. Both panels were by Kenneth Shoesmith.

The bronze double doors in the Main restaurant, by Walter and Donald Gilbert, can also be seen here surrounded by the 'Merrie England' painting by Philip Connard.

Above: the main wheelhouse, showing the telegraphs, steering wheels and the Sperry Mk VIII gyro compass, standing to the right of the wheels.

Below: a corner of the radio control room; there were 4 transmitters – long wave, medium wave and two short wave, plus 8 receivers

Below right: Hairdressing salons were available for all three classes: this picture was of the Cabin Class salon. There was also a beauty parlour.

There were 24 motorised steel lifeboats, each 36 feet long and capable of carrying 145 people. Each carried a wireless, water supplies, emergency food and a compass. All the boats, on gravity davits, could be lowered within one minute.

There were four kitchens – one for the Cabin Class restaurant and associated private dining rooms, one for the Tourist Class, one for Third Class and a kosher kitchen, with over 100 cooks plus their ancillary staff and helpers. All were equipped with all the latest in catering equipment, to enable them to cater for all tastes and requirements. For example, the First Class breakfast menu included 20 cereals, 18 kinds of bread and rolls and 15 types of jam and marmalade. Just some of the stores shipped for each voyage included 20 tons of various meats, 4,000 chickens and ducklings, 20 tons of fish, 70,000 eggs, 4,000 pounds of tea and coffee, 30 tons of potatoes, 40,000 pounds of vegetables, 4,000 gallons of milk, 3 tons of butter, 10,000 pounds of sugar and 2,000 pounds of cheese, whilst the wine cellars kept 10,000 bottles of wine, 60,000 bottles of mineral water, 40,000 bottles of beer, 6,000 gallons of draught beer, 5,000 bottles of spirits, 5,000 cigars and 20,000 packets of cigarettes.

There were over 16,000 items of cutlery and tableware, many off Mauretania when she was scrapped, plus 200,000 items of china, glass and crockery. Linen stocks were held in triplicate – one set in use and the others either side of the Atlantic. A total of 500,000 items included 30,000 sheets, 31,000 pillow slips, 21,000 table cloths, 211,000 mixed towels and 5,500 blankets.

The on-board printing presses produced 12,000 menus every day, as well as a daily paper.

Operating for the first time under her own power, the tugs were used to push, pull and guide the massive liner from the fitting out basin into the riiver Clyde.

Within minutes of leaving the basin, she was stranded across the river from bank to bank, when a gust of wind caught her massive sides. She straddled the river for nearly half an hour before the tugs managed to ease her off. Shortly after this she grounded again, but there was no damage to the hull on either occasion.

Departure day was chosen as Tuesday, 24th March 1936, to take the greatest possible advantage of the high spring tide to help her passage down the Clyde. The minimum amount of fuel needed for her first journey was loaded, and only two lifeboats were fitted in case of emergency. *Queen Mary* was kept as light as possible, even though the the channel had been dredged. About half a million tons of sand and mud were dredged and dumped at sea, and about 5·5 acres of the bank around the mouth of the Cart were cut away.

By 9.30am, *Queen Mary* gave several blasts on her siren – she was ready to start her life. Tugs moved in and began to ease the liner out from the basin – five from the Clyde Shipping Board, plus *Romsey*, a powerful tug brought up specially from Southampton, and *Paladin*, a tug/tender owned by Anchor Line.

Jointly they pulled her, stern first, into the Clyde, before swinging her head round to face seaward. Some twenty minutes of delicate manoeuvring was needed to achieve this. Two skilled local Clyde pilots, Duncan Cameron and John Murchie, were in joint command.

Queen Mary slowly headed down river, under her own power. The tugs were used primarily for guiding her through the narrow channel. As she approached the bend near Dalmuir, she was caught by the freshening wind and swung across the river. Her stern caught briefly on the bank, but the tugs quickly pulled her off; she briefly grounded a second time but again without damage. Both times were, however, sufficient to be listed at Lloyds. The crowds on the banks were close enough to call across to the people on the liner.

Travelling at between six and seven knots, it took *Queen Mary* about four hours to reach open water, off Gourock, arriving at 2.10pm. All the way down the Clyde the banks had been lined with thousands of well-wishers, cheering the newest addition to the merchant navy, and widely regarded as a potent symbol of the end of the Depression.

For the next two days *Queen Mary* was anchored off Gourock. Tests and trials were conducted on much of her equipment on the Wednesday, and her lifeboats were fitted. During that day brief sea trials were run. At night she was fully floodlit, an amazing spectacle for the crowds out to see the new liner. Compass adjustments were made and some preliminary runs and anchor tests were conducted.

In the early hours of Thursday morning, the 26th, she raised her anchors, and sailed south, for Southampton.

In May 1930 Cunard began urging the Southern Railway Company to build a new drydock large enough for the new generation of liners, but they had been resisting. In the end, Sir Percy Bates virtually gave them an ultimatum:

Around 5·5 acres of the bank around the junction with the river Cart had been purchased by the Clyde Navigation Trust so that the channel could be enlarged. Some two miles of the river was dredged and widened; the Trust used a rock breaker and drilling equipment, and even used blasting in places, to ensure the hull would clear the river bed. The total cost for this work was put at over £80,000.

In spite of all this work, and an extremely high tide on the day, in some places there was less than 4 feet clearance between the hull and the river bed.

*In the main picture on the preceding page, Paladin can be seen leading
the new liner on her journey down the Clyde. The two smaller pictures
show Clydesiders crowding the banks on both sides of the river as
they watched the greatest marvel of the century leave their backyard.
As the tugs fussed around her, they gradually manipulated her head
round; finally she was ready to begin her journey to the sea.*

With the tugs providing an escort, Queen Mary slowly passed down the Clyde, until she finally reached open water at Greenock.

Here she anchored, and spent the next two days installing her lifeboats, conducting preliminary equipment checks, making compass adjustments and the thousand-and-one other things needed in a liner fresh out of the shipyard.

At night she was brightly floodlit, creating a beautiful scene for the thousands of spectators on the shore, and creating a lot of business for the local excursion steamers.

As Queen Mary reached Greenock, she passed the burnt-out *L'Atlantique*, waiting to be towed up the Clyde to the breakers.

After a maiden voyage in September 1931, *L'Atlantique* caught fire in the English Channel in January 1933, with the loss of 17 lives and was subsequently declared a total loss.

Below and far right: at Southampton, she entered the King George V drydock, passing Majestic, awaiting scrapping but being used as a grand-stand for spectators.

'build the dock or we move our ships'. In effect they were saying they would ensure the end of Southampton as a major terminus. As a result Southern Railway capitulated, and, with a government grant, built the King George V drydock, at the end of the new dock area then being built on reclaimed land. King George V and Queen Mary had officially opened the drydock on 26th July, 1933, aboard the royal yacht Victoria and Albert.

Queen Mary arrived off Cowes at 7am on Friday, 27th, and anchored in the Roads. Around noon she continued up Southampton Water, and entered the new drydock. The dock gate was closed by 2.45pm, and some 58 million gallons of water pumped out. She was high and dry and sitting on her blocks by 7pm. Over the next few days her bottom was thoroughly cleaned and repainted; fixtures remaining from the launch were removed, and the propellers changed in preparation for the speed trials.

On Sunday the *Queen Mary* was opened to the public. Reports at the time claimed around twenty-five thousand spectators paid a shilling each to view the ship, while many thousands more walked round the dock area viewing the spectacle. Eighteen special trains were laid on, bringing at least 8,000 spectators.

Work was completed by 8th April, 1936, and slowly *Queen Mary* was eased out of the dock and towed across to the Ocean Dock, where she was moored opposite Cunard's famed *Aquitania*. The company could now complete the interior, fitting carpets, furniture and other accoutrements ready to take up her life as the world's most luxurious liner.

Refuelling was completed, and on 15th April she left Southampton. During the next two days various trials were conducted in the Irish Sea, and minor adjustments made to the machinery. Once again she arrived at Gourock, ready to conduct her speed trials on the 18th April. Fourteen runs were made during that day, over the Admiralty measured mile, off the Isle of Arran, on one occasion officially reaching 32·84 knots, well above her designed speed.

David Kirkwood, the MP who had fought so tenaciously for *Queen Mary* to survive during the barren years, was not forgotten. As the liner was completing her runs, Lord Aberconway, the Chairman of John Brown's, sent him a telegram, acknowledging his efforts over the years.

The runs were completed and the liner returned to anchor off Gourock by 6pm, finally heading south around 9.30pm for Southampton. The last carpets were laid, the final items of furniture fitted, the decorations given their finishing touch-ups and the paintwork given one last wipe-over.

At noon on May 12th, 1936, the builder's houseflag was lowered and the Cunard-White Star flag raised.

Queen Mary was now officially part of the Cunard fleet.

Queen Mary docks for the first time beside her consort, Aquitania, in the Ocean Dock, Southampton on 8th April 1936

Facing page: high on her supporting blocks, Queen Mary prepares for the thorough cleaning and repainting of her lower hull

A series of striking photographs of Queen Mary progressing through her various speed and turning trials on the Admiralty measured mile on 18th April 1936. These were passed with amazing ease considering her size. Both John Brown's and Cunard were well pleased at the overall results, especially the performance and stability.

Below: Queen Mary returns to Southampton, to prepare for her maiden voyage

Bibliography: Books that have been read, or just enjoyed.

Ships of the British Merchant Navy	EC Talbot-Booth	Melrose	1932
Queen Mary: A record in pictures	G Blake	Batsford	1936
Merchant Ships	EC Talbot-Booth	Sampson Low	1944
Ships of the Cunard Line	F Dodman	Adlard Coles	1955
Cunard White Star Liners	HM Le Fleming	Ian Allan	1960
The Mary: The Inevitable Ship	N Potter & J Frost	Harrap	1961
The Stateliest Ship	DO Ringwald, et al.	SSHA	1969
When Luxury Went to Sea	D Phillips-Birt	David & Charles	1971
North Atlantic Liner Queen Mary	Liners of the Past series	Patrick Stephens	1972
The Queens of the North Atlantic	R Lacey	Sidgwick & Jackson	1973
The Cunard Line	W Mitchell	WSS	1973
North Atlantic Seaway	NRP Bonsor	Brookside	1975-1980
Cunard and the North Atlantic	F Hyde	Macmillan	1975
The Liners	T Coleman	Penguin	1976
Ocean Liners	R Wall	New Burlington	1977
Grand Days of Travel	C Owen	Windward	1979
Trans-Atlantic Liners	W Miller	Davis & Charles	1981
Beau Voyage: *Life Aboard the Last Great Ships*	JM Brinnin	Bracken	1981
Fifty Famous Liners Vol I	F Braynard & W Miller	Patrick Stephens	1982
Queen Mary: her early years	CWR Winter	Patrick Stephens	1986
The Sway of the Grand Saloon	JM Brinnin	Arlington	1986
Grand Luxe: Trans-Atlantic Style	JM Brinnin	Holt	1988
Queen Mary: 50 years of splendour	DF Hutchings	Kingfisher	1988
Cunard White Star Liners	RP de Kerbrech	Conway Maritime	1988
Flagships of the Line	MH Watson	Patrick Stephens	1988
Queen Mary	R Watton	Conway Maritime	1989
Cunard Portraits	JH Isherwood	World Ship Society	1990
Atlantic Liners of the Cunard Line	N McCart	Patrick Stephens	1990
Great Ocean Liners	I Dear	Batsford	1991
Ocean Steamers	J Adams	New Cavendish	1993
The Atlantic Blue Riband	C Mackenzie-Kennedy	Sessions	1993
Queen Mary	J Steele	Phaidon	1995
Aquitania	L & RA Streater	Maritime Publishing	1997

Sea Breezes: too numerous to list, but enjoyed over many years
and, of course, The Cunard Steamship Company, Limited, for their production of a vast amount of promotional material and ephemera, much still in the public domain.